Contents

Senses

We all have five senses.

The Five Senses

Smelling

Rebecca Rissman

www.raintreepublishers.co.uk
Visit our website to find out more information about Raintree books.

To order:
☎ Phone 0845 6044371
🖨 Fax +44 (0) 1865 312263
📧 Email myorders@raintreepublishers.co.uk

Customers from outside the UK please telephone +44 1865 312262

Raintree is an imprint of Capstone Global Library Limited, a company incorporated in England and Wales having its registered office at 7 Pilgrim Street, London EC4V 6LB – Registered company number: 6695582

Text © Capstone Global Library Limited 2010
First published in hardback in 2010
Paperback edition first published in 2011
The moral rights of the proprietor have been asserted.

Edited by Rebecca Rissman and Catherine Veitch
Designed by Ryan Frieson and Kimberly R. Miracle
Original illustrations © Capstone Global Library
Illustrated by Tony Wilson (pp. 10, 12, 22, 23)
Picture research by Tracy Cummins
Originated by Capstone Global Library
Printed in China by South China Printing Company Ltd

ISBN 978 0 431 19480 6 (hardback)
14 13 12 11 10
10 9 8 7 6 5 4 3 2 1

ISBN 978 0 431 19486 8 (paperback)
15 14 13 12 11
10 9 8 7 6 5 4 3 2 1

British Library Cataloguing in-Publication Data
Rissman, Rebecca
Smelling. - (The Five Senses)
612.8'6--dc22
A full catalogue record for this book is available from the British Library.

Acknowledgments
The author and publishers are grateful to the following for permission to reproduce copyright material: Corbis pp. **9** (© Tom Stewart), **17** (© moodboard), **18** (© Peter Turnley); Getty Images pp. **4** (Werner Dieterich), **6** (Burke/Triolo Productions), **7** (JJ), **11** (CO2), **13** (arabianEye), **14** (Johannes Rodach), **15** (Andreanna Seymore), **16** (VEER/Steve Cicero); PhotoEdit Inc. p. **19** (© David Young-Wolff); Photolibrary p. **20** (Jupiterimages); Shutterstock pp. **5** (© svitlana10), **8** (© Rafal Olechowski), **23 B** (© Rafal Olechowski), **23 C** (© svitlana10); Tom Pantages Photography p. **21** (© Tom Pantages).

Cover photograph of a boy smelling a flower reproduced with permission of Shutterstock (© zhuda). Back cover photograph of a girl smelling a flower reproduced with permission of Shutterstock (© Rafal Olechowski).

The publishers would like to thank Nancy Harris, Yael Biederman, and Matt Siegel for their assistance in the preparation of this book.

Every effort has been made to contact copyright holders of any material reproduced in this book. Any omissions will be rectified in subsequent printings if notice is given to the publisher.

We use our senses every day.

Smelling and seeing are senses.

Tasting, touching, and hearing are also senses.

How do you smell?

You use your nose to smell.

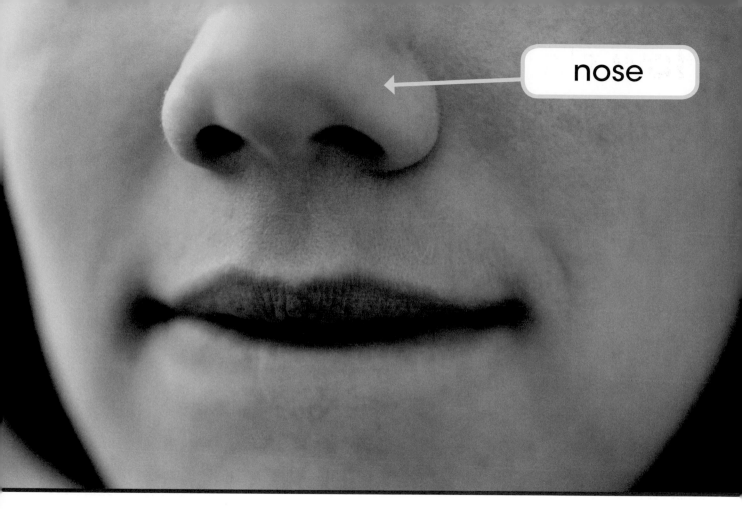

nose

Your nose is on your face.

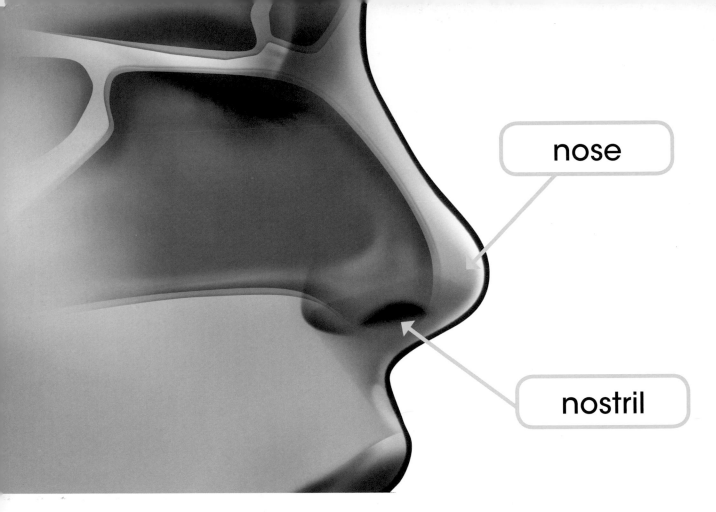

nose

nostril

You breathe air into your nose through nostrils.

Your nose smells things in the air.

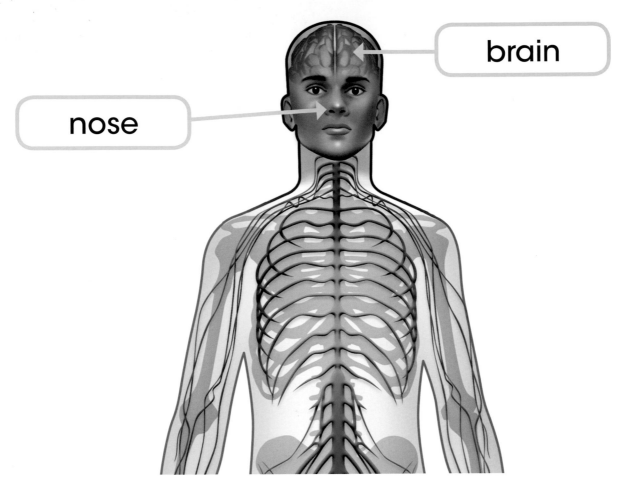

brain

nose

Your nose sends messages to your brain.

Your brain tells you what you
are smelling.

What do you smell?

You can smell plants.

You can smell animals.

You can smell food cooking.

You can smell flowers.

Smell can protect you

You can smell smoke.

You can smell things that are rotten.

Unsafe smells

Some smells are bad for you.
Smelling some glues can make
you sick.

Smelling some paints can make you sick.

Naming the parts you use to smell

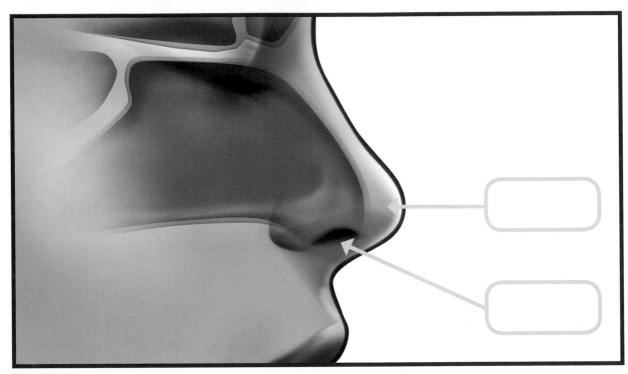

Point to where these labels should go.

nose   nostril

Answer on page 10.

Picture glossary

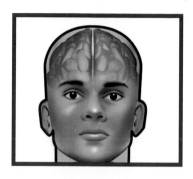

brain part of your body inside your head that helps you think, remember, feel, and move

nostril one of two holes in your nose where air goes in and out

sense something that helps you smell, see, touch, taste, or hear things around you

Index

Note to parents and teachers

Before reading

Explain to children that people use five senses to understand the world: seeing, hearing, tasting, touching, and smelling. Tell children that there are different body parts associated with each sense. Then ask children which body part they think they use to smell. Tell children that they use their nose to smell.

After reading

• Show children the diagram of the nose on page 22. Ask them to point to where the label "nostril" should go.

• Get the children to take it in turns wearing a blindfold and having a selection of things to smell. Can they guess what they are smelling?

• Make a list of smells that children like, and a list of smells they do not like. Ask children if they think bad smells act as a warning. Explain that some smells, such as smoke or rotten food warn them of danger.